43

First published 2000 by Walker Books Ltd
87 Vauxhall Walk, London SE11 5HJ

2 4 6 8 10 9 7 5 3 1

© this selection
Centre for Language in Primary Education,
London Borough of Southwark
Text and illustrations © publication date
individual authors and illustrators
Cover illustration © 1994 Cathie Felstead

This book has been typeset in Columbus MT.

Printed in Hong Kong

British Library Cataloguing in Publication Data
A catalogue record for this book is
available from the British Library.

ISBN 0-7445-6799-8 (hb)
ISBN 0-7445-6998-2 (pb)

The Sun is Laughing

A Collection of Poems
chosen by Sue Ellis

WALKER BOOKS
AND SUBSIDIARIES
LONDON · BOSTON · SYDNEY

Acknowledgements

Except for **"Hopping frog, hop here and be seen"**, the poems in this book are all taken from collections published by Walker Books:

Throwing a Tree and **Birdfoot's Grampa** are taken from *Anthology for the Earth*, edited by Judy Allen.

Isn't My Name Magical?, **Sun Is Laughing**, **For Forest**, **'Bye Now** and **Goodbye Now** are taken from *A Caribbean Dozen*, edited by John Agard and Grace Nichols.

Ozymandias is taken from *Classic Poetry: An Illustrated Collection*, selected by Michael Rosen.

The limericks on pages 24–25 are taken from *I Never Saw a Purple Cow*.

The Crab that Writes and **Mammoth** are taken from *Moon Frog*.

Over My Toes is taken from *Tea in the Sugar Bowl, Potato in My Shoe*.

I Have an Oasis and **How Many Stars?** are taken from *There's an Awful Lot of Weirdos in Our Neighbourhood*.

Walker Books is grateful for permission to reproduce the following:

"Birdfoot's Grampa" by Joseph Bruchac from *Entering Onondaga*.

"'Bye Now/Goodbye Now" from *When I Dance* © James Berry 1988. Reprinted by permission of The Peters Fraser and Dunlop Group Limited on behalf of: JAMES BERRY.

"Isn't My Name Magical?" from *Isn't My Name Magical?* © James Berry. Reprinted by permission of The Peters Fraser and Dunlop Group Limited on behalf of: JAMES BERRY.

"The Sun Is Laughing" from *Give Yourself a Hug* (A & C Black [Publishers] Ltd, 1994) and "For Forest" from *Come On Into My Tropical Garden* (A & C Black [Publishers] Ltd, 1998). Reproduced with permission of Curtis Brown Ltd, London, on behalf of Grace Nichols, Copyright Grace Nichols 1988, 1994.

Contents

Isn't My Name Magical?

Nobody can see my name on me.
My name is inside
and all over me, unseen
like other people also keep it.
Isn't my name magical?

My name is mine only.
It tells I am individual,
the one special person it shakes
when I'm wanted.

Even if someone else answers
for me, my message hangs in air
haunting others, till it stops
with me, the right name.
Isn't your name and my name magic?

If I'm with hundreds of people
and my name gets called,
my sound switches me on to answer
like it was my human electricity.

My name echoes across playground,
it comes, it demands my attention.
I have to find out who calls,
who wants me for what.
My name gets blurted out in class,
it is terror, at a bad time,
because somebody is cross.

My name gets called in a whisper
I am happy, because
my name may have touched me
with a loving voice.
Isn't your name and my name magic?

James Berry

The Crab that Writes

When the tide is low on moonlit nights,
Out of the sea crawls the crab that writes,
Out of the sea crawls the crab whose claw
Writes these words on the shining shore:

> *Pebble mussel*
> *Fin and scale*
> *Sole and mackerel*
> *Skate and whale*
> *Seaweed starfish*
> *Salt and stone*
> *Sand and shell and cuttlebone.*

When the tide is low on moonlit nights,
Back to the sea crawls the crab that writes,
Back to the sea crawls the crab whose claw
Leaves these words on the shining shore:

Pebble mussel
Fin and scale
Sole and mackerel
Skate and whale
Seaweed starfish
Salt and stone
Sand and shell and cuttlebone.

Richard Edwards

Sun Is Laughing

This morning she got up
on the happy side of bed,
pulled back
the grey sky-curtains
and poked her head
through the blue window
of heaven,
her yellow laughter
spilling over,
falling broad across the grass,
brightening the washing on the line,
giving more shine
to the back of a ladybug
and buttering up all the world.

Then, without any warning,
as if she was suddenly bored,
or just got sulky
because she could hear no one
giving praise
to her shining ways,
Sun slammed the sky-window close,
plunging the whole world
into greyness once more.

O Sun, moody one,
how can we live
without the holiday of your face?

Grace Nichols

I Have an Oasis

I have an oasis,
It's up in the clouds
Away from the rush
And the roar of the crowds,
Away from the pushing
And pulling and pain,
Away from the sadness
And anger and strain,
Away from the envy
And cheating and greed,
Away from the pressure –
What more could I need?
I grow my geraniums
And lettuce that's curled,
In my little garden
On top of the world.

Colin McNaughton

14

Over My Toes

Over my toes
goes

the soft sea wash

see the sea wash

the soft sand slip

see the sea slip

the soft sand slide

see the sea slide

the soft sand slap

see the sea slap

the soft sand wash

over my toes.

Michael Rosen

Mammoth

Once the snow stood on my back,
Once I was colossal,
Once my feet made glaciers crack,
Now I'm just a fossil.

Once I trumpeted and heard
Echoes ring the plain,
Once I felt returning spring
Changing snow to rain.

Once I waved my wild tusks high,
Once I was colossal,
Now I never see the sky,
Now I'm just a fossil.

Richard Edwards

Ozymandias

I met a traveller from an antique land
Who said: Two vast and trunkless legs of stone
Stand in the desert. Near them, on the sand,
Half sunk, a shattered visage lies, whose frown,
And wrinkled lip, and sneer of cold command,
Tell that its sculptor well those passions read
Which yet survive (stamped on these lifeless things),
The hand that mocked them and the heart that fed;
And on the pedestal these words appear:
"My name is Ozymandias, king of kings;
Look on my works, ye Mighty, and despair!"
Nothing beside remains. Round the decay
Of that colossal wreck, boundless and bare,
The lone and level sands stretch far away.

Percy Bysshe Shelley

Throwing a Tree

The two executioners stalk along over the knolls,
Bearing two axes with heavy heads shining and wide,
And a long limp two-handled saw toothed for cutting great boles,
And so they approach the proud tree that bears
   the death mark on its side.

Jackets doffed they swing axes and chop away just above ground,
And the chips fly about and lie white on the moss and fallen leaves;
Till a broad deep gash in the bark is hewn all the way round,
And one of them tries to hook upwards a rope,
   which at last he achieves.

The saw then begins, till the top of the tall giant shivers:
The shivers are seen to grow greater at each cut than before:
They edge out the saw, tug the rope; but the tree only quivers,
And kneeling and sawing again, they step back to try
   pulling once more.

Then, lastly, the living mast sways, further sways: with a shout
Job and Ike rush aside. Reached the end of its long staying powers
The tree crashes downward: it shakes all its neighbours throughout,
And two hundred years' steady growth has been ended
   in less than two hours.

Thomas Hardy

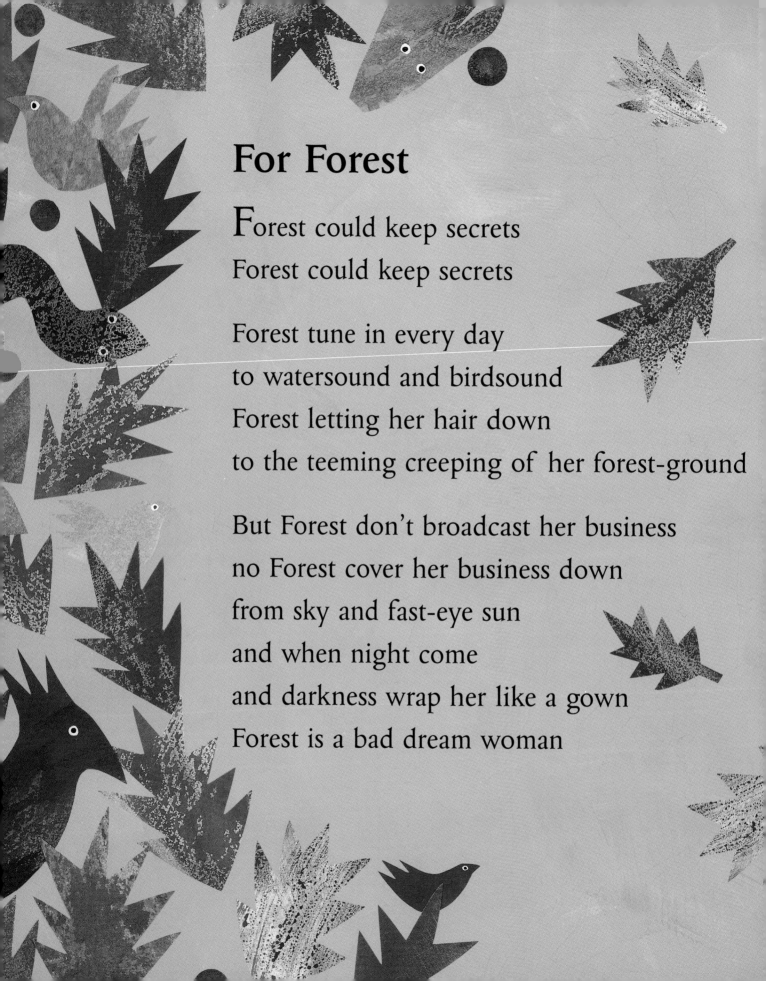

For Forest

Forest could keep secrets
Forest could keep secrets

Forest tune in every day
to watersound and birdsound
Forest letting her hair down
to the teeming creeping of her forest-ground

But Forest don't broadcast her business
no Forest cover her business down
from sky and fast-eye sun
and when night come
and darkness wrap her like a gown
Forest is a bad dream woman

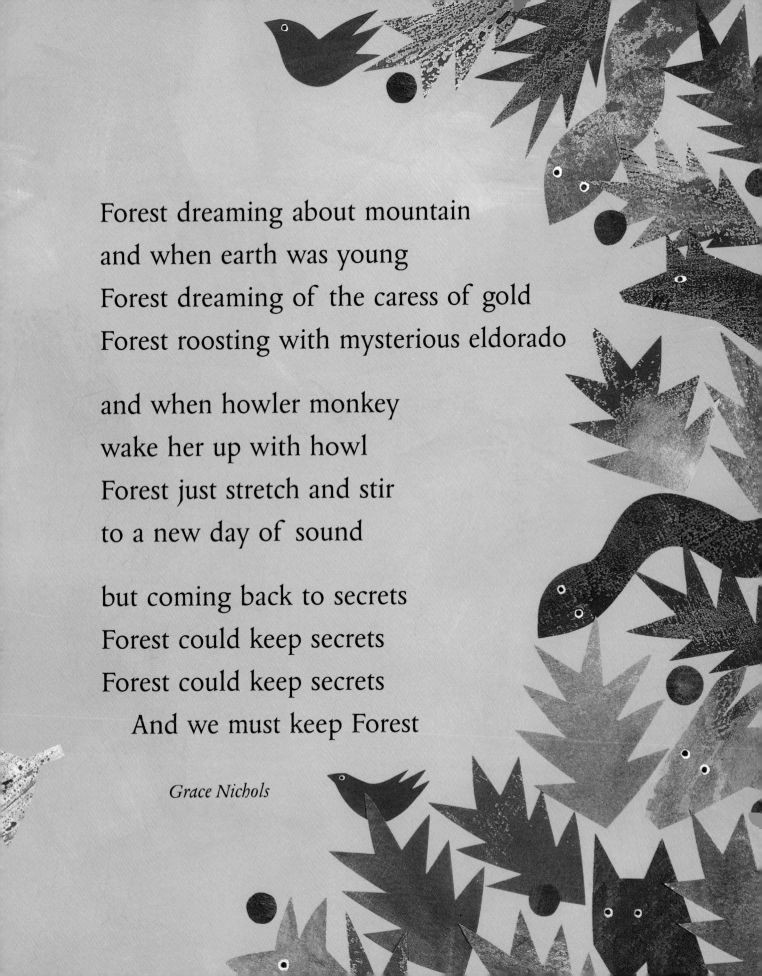

Forest dreaming about mountain
and when earth was young
Forest dreaming of the caress of gold
Forest roosting with mysterious eldorado

and when howler monkey
wake her up with howl
Forest just stretch and stir
to a new day of sound

but coming back to secrets
Forest could keep secrets
Forest could keep secrets
      And we must keep Forest

Grace Nichols

Birdfoot's Grampa

The old man
must have stopped our car
two dozen times to climb out
and gather into his hands
the small toads blinded
by our light and leaping,
live drops of rain.

      The rain was falling,
      a mist about his white hair
      and I kept saying
      you can't save them all,
      accept it, get back in
      we've got places to go.

But, leathery hands full
of wet brown life,
knee deep in the summer
roadside grass,
he just smiled and said
they have places to go, too.

Joseph Bruchac

Hopping frog, hop here and be seen,
I'll not pelt you with stick or stone:
Your cap is laced and your coat is green;
Goodbye, we'll let each other alone.

Christina Rossetti

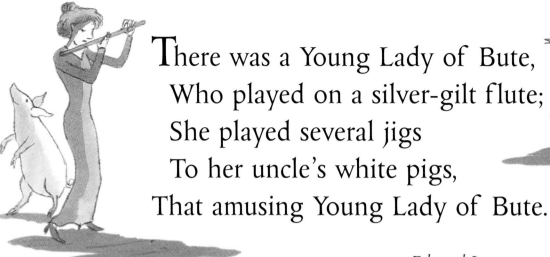

There was a Young Lady of Bute,
  Who played on a silver-gilt flute;
    She played several jigs
    To her uncle's white pigs,
  That amusing Young Lady of Bute.

Edward Lear

There was an Old Man with a beard
Who said, "It is just as I feared! –
    Four Larks and a Wren,
    Two Owls and a Hen,
Have all built their nests in my beard!"

Edward Lear

There was a young man of Bengal
Who went to a fancy-dress ball,
 He went, just for fun,
 Dressed up as a bun,
And a dog ate him up in the hall.

Anonymous

There was an Old Man on the Border,
Who lived in the utmost disorder;
 He danced with the Cat
 And made Tea in his Hat,
Which vexed all the folks on the Border.

Edward Lear

How Many Stars?

When I was a boy I would ask my dad:
"How many stars are there hanging in the sky?"
"More than enough, son,
More than I could say.
Enough to keep you counting
Till your dying day."

When I was a boy I would ask my dad:
"How many fishes are there swimming in the sea?"
"More than enough, son,
More than I could say.
Enough to keep you counting
Till your dying day."

When I was a boy I would ask my dad:
"How many creepy-crawlies are there in the world?"
"More than enough, son.
More than I could say.
Enough to keep you counting
Till your dying day."

It seemed like there wasn't anything my dad didn't know.

Colin McNaughton

'Bye Now

Walk good
   Walk good
Noh mek macca go juk yu
Or cow go buk yu.
Noh mek dog bite yu
Or hungry go ketch yu, yah!

Noh mek sunhot turn yu dry.
No mek rain soak yu.
Noh mek tief tief yu.
Or stone go buck yu foot, yah!
   Walk good
      Walk good

James Berry

Goodbye Now

Walk well
Walk well
Don't let thorns run in you
Or let a cow butt you.
Don't let a dog bite you
Or hunger catch you, hear!

Don't let sun's heat turn you dry.
Don't let rain soak you.
Don't let a thief rob you
Or a stone bump your foot, hear!
Walk well
Walk well

James Berry

List of Illustrators